Daniel in the Lions' Den

Based on Daniel 6:4–23

By Mrs. Marvin Good

Illustrated by Lester M. Miller

Rod and Staff Publishers, Inc.
P.O. Box 3, Hwy. 172
Crockett, Kentucky 41413
Telephone: (606) 522-4348

SAY-IT-AGAIN SERIES

Bread and Fish
Daniel in the Lions' Den
David and Goliath
The Good Samaritan
How God Made the World
My Book About Bartimaeus
A Shepherd Boy

These books were written to provide simple, repetitious stories to be read by beginning readers who can profit by the extra repetition, or to be read to younger children whose minds can more readily grasp the content of oft-repeated material.

Copyright, 1993
By
Rod and Staff Publishers, Inc.
Crockett, Kentucky 41413

Printed in U.S.A.
ISBN 978-07399-0006-2
Catalog no. 2396

This is Daniel.
Daniel prayed.
He liked to pray.
Daniel prayed to God.

Look and see.

See Daniel praying.

Daniel knelt by the window.

Daniel knelt by the window to pray.

Daniel knelt by the window to pray.

He prayed by the open window.

Daniel prayed to God.

He gave thanks to God.

Daniel prayed.

He prayed to God every day.

Daniel prayed to God every morning.

He prayed at noon.

He prayed in the evening.

Daniel prayed to God 3 times every day.

The presidents and princes talked.

The presidents and princes talked together.

They talked about Daniel.

The presidents and princes were unkind men.

The presidents and princes did not like Daniel.

They tried to find fault.

They tried to find fault with Daniel.

They could not find fault with him.

Daniel was faithful.
He was faithful to God.
The presidents and princes could find no fault with Daniel.
They did not like Daniel.

The presidents and princes had a plan.

They had a plan to catch Daniel.

They told the king.

The presidents and princes told the king their plan.

"King, O King.

You are great.

Everyone must worship you.

Everyone must worship you, not God."

Daniel prayed.

Daniel obeyed God, not man.

Daniel prayed often.

He prayed 3 times a day.

"We are taking you to the lions' den," said the presidents and princes.

They threw Daniel into the lions' den.

Daniel prayed to God.

Daniel prayed to God when he was in the lions' den.

God sent an angel to Daniel.

The angel shut the lions' mouths.

The angel did not let the lions hurt Daniel.

The angel shut the lions' mouths.

Daniel was glad the angel shut the lions' mouths.

He thanked God for His care.

The king.

The king came to the den.

The king came to see Daniel.

The king was sad.

The king was sad because Daniel was in the lions' den.

He wanted to take Daniel out.

The king came to the den to see Daniel.

"Daniel, Daniel!

"Are you alive, Daniel?" the king called.

"Yes, I am alive," said Daniel.

The king was glad.

The king was very glad.

"The angel came.

The angel came and shut the lions' mouths," said Daniel.

"God was good to me.

God was very good to me."

The king talked to his men. He said, "Take Daniel out."

The king said, "Take Daniel out of the den."

Daniel was happy.

God was good to Daniel.

God was very good to Daniel.

Daniel loved God.

Daniel prayed to God.
He prayed every day.
Daniel prayed 3 times a day.

"We ought to obey God rather than men" (Acts 5:29).